Dear World, I Stutter:

A Series of Open Letters
From a Person Who Stutters

JAMES HAYDEN

Dedicated to those on this journey with me.

Table of Contents

Introduction

The Past

The Present

Family

Relationships

Stuttering Community

Individuals

Introduction

My Story

My story begins at the age of 5 when I first began stuttering and started going to speech therapy. When I first started speech therapy, I was far from fluent; however, over the next 7 years I became more fluent and rarely stuttered. I was extremely fluent from the ages of 12 to 18. No one could tell that I stuttered and I did not consider myself a person that stuttered. When I started my senior year of high school, my stutter returned. My parents and I attributed my stutter returning to excitement and nerves about all of the changes that I would be experiencing in the next year, but I would return to fluency once I became acclimated to my new environment. That didn't happen and over the next two years I ignored the fact that I stuttered and did not talk about it. After the encouragement of my parents and my uncle, I looked into what speech therapy options, if any, my college offered. They offered speech therapy and I went during my junior and senior years of college. Over those two years I became more fluent, but more importantly began the process of accepting the fact that I stutter and probably would for the rest of my life. After I graduated college, I got involved with my local chapter of the National Stuttering Association (NSA). My time in the NSA has helped me tremendously in embracing my stutter, accepting my stutter, growing in self-confidence, and becoming an advocate for stuttering and those that stutter.

To the Reader

Dear Reader,

First, thank you for buying this book. Regardless of your experience with stuttering, I hope this book provides you some insight into what it means to stutter. Each person that stutters has an unique story and perspective about stuttering. Not every person that stutters shares the same views on the topic and that's okay. My story is different than their story and that's beautiful.

If you are a person that stutters, remember you were, are, and always will be more than your stutter. You are not alone in this journey.

If you are a friend or relative of a person who stutters, don't treat them any differently. Be there for them when they need it, but let them find their own voice and speak for themselves. Let them dictate how stuttering works in your relationship.

If you are in the speech pathology field, I hope this book gives a better understanding of the mental, emotional, and psychological aspects of stuttering.

If have no experience with stuttering or have never met a person that stutters, I hope this book gives you an understanding of what stuttering is, but more importantly that it does not define the person. Stuttering is what happens when we talk, but it is not who we are.

Thank you,

James

The Past

To 10 Year Old Me

Dear James,

What's up, dude? This is you fourteen years from now. At this current time in your life, the fourth grade is almost over, you have a good group of friends, and you still stutter; however, you're becoming more fluent as the years pass. I won't tell you most of what happens over the next fourteen years, but I will tell you this: you will be very fluent in two years, will stop speech therapy, will rarely stutter, and neither you nor others will consider you as a person that stutters. All of the self-doubts, questions, and insecurities will disappear with your stutter. You will no longer consider yourself a person who stutters, but a person who used to stutter. However, this period of fluency (fortunately) lasts only a few years. You're thinking, how is this fortunate? My stutter coming back is the furthest thing from fortunate. Allow me to explain.

You start stuttering again your senior year of high school. When this happens mom, dad, and you will attribute it to the nerves and excitement of graduating high school and moving to a new state to begin your college career. We figure your stutter will disappear when you get acclimated to your new surroundings, but your stutter comes to college with you and stays friends with you for all four years. In addition to your stutter, all self-doubts and insecurities you had growing up return. Also, the questions of, "Will any girl be able to see past my stutter?" "How does this impact future job prospects?" "Am I the only person that stutters?" return. Your way of handling the fact that you stutter, completely ignoring the fact and not talking about it, also goes to college with you. Fortunately, you learn how to better handle your stutter and the fact that you stutter when you back to speech therapy.

You go back to speech therapy when you are a junior in college and 20 years old. This is a difficult process to begin because it means admitting to yourself that you do stutter. A hard thing to do because 20 year old you is prideful. Ultimately, your pride begins to fade and over the next two years all of your self-doubts and insecurities fade away and feelings of acceptance and ownership take their place. This leads you to embracing the fact that you stutter by admitting you're back in speech therapy, talking about it with friends and family, writing about your journey with stuttering, and sharing articles about stuttering on social media (you'll learn what that means in a few years). However, the three questions you cling to are not answered in the therapy room, but rather through the life experiences.

The first question you hold and continue to hold as you get older is, "Will a girl be able to see past my stutter?" The answer is yes. You meet her a few months before you go back to speech therapy. It ultimately does not end the way you thought it would, but good things come from it. She teaches you to embrace the small victories of life and your stutter. This is told to you numerous times during speech therapy, but she's the first person that shows you how to embrace the victories. She teaches you to be comfortable about your stutter with you people you don't know all that well or for a long period of time. But most importantly, she shows you that a girl can see James for James and not see James as that guy that stutters.

Your stutter does not impact future jobs because you won't let it. You have the same summer job for seven summers, some summers you stutter and others you don't. Regardless of your fluency levels, your co-workers and bosses treat you the same and don't let your stutter influence their decisions. When you are 20 and two months away from re-entering speech therapy, you work at an all-boys summer camp. This will be the best job you have because of the lessons you learn about life and stuttering during that summer. I won't tell you those lessons, you'll learn those in 10 years. When you graduate you land a job in your field relatively quickly. At this point in life, you've accepted and embraced the fact that you stutter (for the most part) and it doesn't hold you back from doing what you want to do. You also use this job to educate people about stuttering through conversations with your co-workers

As you get older, you realize that you are not the only person on earth that stutters. Yet, you do not meet another person who stutters until you're 22, a few months out of college, and join the local chapter of the National Stuttering Association (NSA). I know it sounds weird that something like this actually exists, but it does. For the first time in your life, you will be around people who truly get it. They will challenge you on your views of stuttering and you challenge them. This group will tremendously increase your confidence in yourself and in your stutter, will give you opportunities you never thought would happen, and make you do things 18 year old you never thought you would do.

I know I make stuttering sound not that bad and it isn't, but I'm not going to lie to you. There are some instances when people don't think you can or should give a presentation, be a tour guide, or do anything else that involves public speaking because of the fact that you stutter. That will make you mad to no end, but use it as motivation to prove them wrong. You ultimately do. There will be times when people laugh at your stutter. Be mad, but use it as an opportunity to teach. When someone accuses you of lying because you're stuttering on a word, stutter on and teach them that you're not a liar.

You don't realize this now, but you've got a great support system of family and friends who will be on this journey with you. It will be hard to let them in at times, but let them in.

Just remember one thing: You always were, always are, and always will be so much more than your stutter. I know you may not see that now, but in time you will. Trust me.

Yours,

James

The Present

Family

To My Parents

Dear Mom and Dad,

Words are inadequate to express my gratitude towards y'all, but they're the best I got. Thank you for your constant, unwavering, and unconditional support on my journey with stuttering.

During my childhood, thank you for taking me to my numerous speech therapy sessions. Thank you for making sure what I practiced at speech therapy went home with us and wasn't left behind. Thank you for consoling me when stuttering won or a kid picked on me because I stuttered, but more importantly thank you for encouraging me and celebrating the small victories of fluency with me. Thank you for standing up for me when I was too mad or upset to use my own voice, but thank you for letting me use my own voice during every other occasion.

As I entered college and my stutter came back, thank you for encouraging me to go back to speech therapy. Although I ignored your words for two years, going back was ultimately one of the best things I've ever done. Although I still stutter, speech therapy helped me with something far more important: acceptance. If it wasn't for y'all's encouragement to back to therapy, I know I wouldn't be where I am today in my journey with stuttering.

Now that I'm out of college and speech therapy, thank you for encouraging and supporting my journey with stuttering and the route it is now taking. One way is by supporting my involvement with the NSA. This is done by attending Baton Rouge NSA chapter's first open house and encouraging and supporting my decision to go to my first NSA conference. Another way is by allowing me to dictate my how and when we talk about my journey with stuttering. It took me many years to get to this point, but I'm glad we can now have open and honest conversations about stuttering and all that comes with it.

Most importantly thank you for seeing me as your son and not your son that stutters. Thank you for never making my stutter an issue, regardless of my fluency. I know not everyone is fortunate enough to have that kind of support. I now realize how blessed and fortunate I am to have y'all as my parents and my support system.

Love always,

James

To My Sister

Dear Jessica,

I know I've embarrassed you numerous times over the past 21 years, but thank you for never letting my stutter be one of the things that has embarrassed you. Thank you for seeing me as your protective, aggravating, and all the other adjectives you have used to describe me brother and not as your stuttering brother. Thank you for letting me speak for myself in all instances, but also stepping in when needed. When we mess with and pick on one another, thanks for not going there and making fun of my stutter, even in jest. That speaks highly of your character.

You got a bright future ahead of you, Jess. I know I don't tell you this often enough, but I'm proud of you. Keep on doing what you're doing.

Love,

James

To My Family

Dear Family,

Throughout my life, y'all have always been there for me. From summer cabbage ball games to graduations to life advice to helping me move and everything else in between, I know I can always count on y'all to be there for me and help in any way possible. Over the past year and a half, I have realized that y'all have always been influential figures in my journey with stuttering.

When I first began to stutter and continued to until high school, thank you for seeing it as a part of me and not me. Thank you for taking me to speech therapy when my parents couldn't do it. When my stutter returned, after my short visit with fluency, thank you for not mentioning the return of my long lost friend. Thank you for allowing me to set the tone on when and how we talked about stuttering.

As I have graduated from college and joined the workforce, thank you for your support in this new chapter of my life. Thank you for supporting my writings and encouraging me to continue writing. Thank you for not brushing away the NSA, but instead taking interest in it and asking me about my meetings, what the NSA is about, and supporting my attendance in it.

Mainly, thank you for seeing me as your nephew or cousin and not your stuttering nephew or cousin.

Love,

James

To My Uncle Who Helped Me Realize I Need

To Go Back to Speech Therapy

Dear Wayne,

I was on Spring Break during my sophomore year of college. You invited me to go to the New Orleans Pelicans game with you something we've done many times, but this time was different. On the way to the game, the topic of me going back to speech therapy suddenly came up. I don't know why you mentioned I should look into going back to speech therapy out of the blue, but thank you. At that moment on Airline Highway, I thought, "Oh crap. Mom and dad are right. Maybe I need to see what USM has to offer." Instead of focusing on the Pelicans game that night, I focused on your words. For two years, I ignored the words of my parents because I didn't want to admit that they were right, but your words were a wakeup call. It took hearing the same words, but a different voice, to make me realize that this was something I needed to do. The next week I heeded your words and the words of my parents and looked into speech therapy.

Had you not mentioned it, I know I would've continued to ignore my stutter and my parents' suggestion to seek out therapy. I would still be lying to myself about the fact that I'm ok with my stutter. If you never mentioned speech therapy, I don't know where I would be, but I do know I wouldn't have the confidence in myself and in my stutter that I do today.

Thanks again, Franchise.

James

Relationships

To the First Girl to See Past My Stutter

Dear Brooke**,

When we first met, I was a few months shy of returning to speech therapy. I was a bundle of nerves and full of apprehension about that fact. All of the doubts, second guesses, and questions I thought had put to bed many years ago were now up and roaming my mind. One of the biggest questions I've had since a young age was, "Can a girl see past the fact that I stutter?" You see, I knew I was not the only person that stuttered, but I didn't know anyone else who stuttered and as a result didn't see or know of any relationships involving a person who stutters and a person who doesn't stutter.

As the months progressed, we became closer and I was beginning the process of accepting the fact that I stutter and would probably do so for the rest of my life. Although we were getting closer, the elephant in the room was still there and intentionally ignored. That began to change on that cool Friday night in November when you asked me to your sorority's winter formal. At that moment, you answered the question I long held with a resounding, "Yes!" I was at peace that night and put that question back to bed.

The dance ultimately didn't happen, but we did spend a lot of time together between that November night and the beginning of the spring semester. During that time, I opened up a lot to you about my journey with stuttering, something I previously did with only the closest of close friends. I did this because it felt right and I thought if this were to be something you needed to know about my biggest insecurity, at that time.

As the spring semester progressed, I realized that what I thought was there wasn't. It was difficult to accept and it took a couple of years to get over the resentment and anger I harbored towards you. I spent many nights thinking of the hows and whys of what happened. I placed a lot of blame on you, but the more I replayed everything the more I realized I was at fault too. I consider myself to be a good reader of people and my read on you was originally wrong. As a result, I was mad at myself for allowing what happened to happen and allowing myself to open up to someone who I hadn't known for years. You were the personification of that self-anger. Every time I saw you over a two year period I was reminded of how I felt like I was led like a sheep to the slaughter and played like a fiddle. But, as the year since we reconciled and I reconciled with myself passed, I realized you never intended to hurt me. I have gotten more comfortable with the fact that I stutter and opening up about it and no longer resent you for what happened. Although there was a lot of hurt in the hows and whys of what happened, in hindsight I can see the beauty in it.

By opening up to you about stuttering, in your car on that December night, I became more comfortable talking about my stutter with people who I may not have known for a long time. That conversation allowed me to put into words what was on my mind about stuttering. You re-taught me how to enjoy and celebrate the small victories I had with stuttering, a skill I had long since forgotten. I remember one Sunday night in particular when I read the readings at Mass fluently. Later that night, you pulled me aside to hug me and tell me how proud of me you were. I responded with, "We don't need to make a Broadway production out of this," because I did what I expected of myself. In looking back at the night, it was the first time I saw in action what my speech therapists had been telling me for a while, "James, learn to celebrate the small victories." Thanks for putting into action those words and re-teaching me how to enjoy and celebrate the small victories not only with stuttering, but in life. Lastly, thank you for teaching me that a girl can see past my stutter. That puts 10 year old, 18 year old, 24 year old, and future James at peace.

All the Best,

James

** Name changed

To My Friends

Dear Friends,

When I first met each of you, I was at different points of my journey with stuttering. For those that I met when during my fluent years, thank you for not letting the return of my old friend impact our friendship. For those that met me when I originally stuttered or when it returned, thank you for seeing past the stutter that introduced me. Regardless of when you met me, thank you for not treating me any differently.

To my friends I made in college, especially my friends from the Catholic Student Association and the guys from camp, thank you for your constant support. The friendships I formed with each of you were during my most trying time on my journey with stuttering. College was a massive time of transition for me. During my college career, I went from ignoring my stutter to starting to embrace and accept it. Some days were harder than others and thank you for being there during the good, bad, and ugly. Thank you for being there to make me appreciate and celebrate the small victories of stuttering, while also being there when I needed to vent about the journey. Thank you for the tough love call outs that I needed when I let the fact that I stutter get the better of me. These calmed me down and helped me towards my journey of acceptance.

To those I confided in about going back to speech therapy, thank you for not breaking that trust. For me going back to speech therapy was a big deal, but thank you for helping me realize going back to speech therapy was not as big of a deal as I made it out to be. It's taken me years to realize that, but thank you for planting that idea in my head.

I realize how fortunate and lucky I am to have friends that see James and not James the stutterer.

Thank you for your friendship,

James

To Camp Abbey

Dear Camp Abbey,

It's weird that we are such good friends. The first time I heard about you, I wanted nothing to do with you. I heard about you a year later and I hesitantly accepted your friendship because I thought we wouldn't get along. Four years later, I'm glad I accepted your friendship because of all that you taught me about life and stuttering. The life lessons are for another day and another letter, but the lessons that you taught me about stuttering still stick with me today. They are:

1. I Care About My Stutter More Than Others Do

During the first hour of our friendship, one of the campers went up to my co-counselor, Brad, and asked, "Hey Brad, does James stutter?" Brad's response was, "Ask him." The camper then proceeded to ask me and I said, "Yes." The camper's response was, "Cool, so does my sister," and he moved on with his life. That moment taught me that if he doesn't care, then why should I care that I stutter.

2. Own Who You Are

Every week, we would receive a new batch of campers and every week I was given a new group of campers. As a result, Brad and I had to go over your rules and regulations of camp and our cabin, but more importantly it required me to announce something that I wanted to hide from the world: "I'm James and I stutter." At that time, I was a few short months away from going back to speech therapy and I was still running from my stutter. I knew I had to tell my campers this fact about myself because I would be with them 24/7 for the next week and they may not understand if I didn't tell them. When I said, "I'm James and I stutter," during the first week of camp it was one of the first times I owned the fact that I stutter to a room full of strangers, kids no less. As the weeks progressed and the weeks turned into years, this statement as become easier to say when I am with a new group of people.

3. **Stuttering is a Great Teacher**

When I introduced myself to my campers every week I followed up "I'm James and I stutter" with, "Some people are tall and some people are short. We all have differences, but we all respect each other and treat one another with kindness." I hope that my speech taught my young campers about embracing and owning their differences, embracing the differences of others, and that one treats everyone with kindness and respect, regardless of what one's appearance or voice.

4. **The Beginnings of Acceptance**

The biggest lesson my time as a camp counselor taught me was acceptance. Our friendship started me on my journey to accepting the fact that I stutter.

Thanks for the lessons,

James

To My Co-Workers

Dear Co-Workers,

I'll break this down into three main categories: my first ever job, the guys at camp, and those at the lab.

To those from my first job, y'all knew me in both my fluent days and non-fluent days. On my non-fluent days, thank you for stepping in when a customer wouldn't believe me because they equated stuttering with lying. Thank you for allowing me to use my voice to assist customers, instead of having me work in the back of the store.

To the guys at camp, thanks for some great summers and fantastic memories. More importantly, thank you for being a part of this journey. Thank you for allowing me to set the tone of how I talk about stuttering with the campers and for y'all following suit. When campers asked you why I stutter thank you for explaining that's just how I talk, instead of being upset with them. When you saw a camper mimic my stutter, thank you for using that as an opportunity to teach him about respect and differences in others and not an opportunity to discipline him. By doing this, you helped me instill into our campers a positive view of those who stutter and how we respect everyone, regardless of our differences.

To my co-workers at the lab, thank you for not letting my stutter impact the way you view me. Within weeks of me starting at the lab, I was chosen to announce the winners of our annual raffle at our Employee Appreciation Day lunch. Between the time I was told I was doing this and the time I announced the names, a million thoughts raced through my head. The main thought being, "What will those that don't know that I stutter think of me once they find out I stutter?" After I announced the winners, I was mad and upset at what happened. I was mad and upset not because I stuttered, but because my stutter was able to introduce itself to y'all before I could introduce myself to y'all. I'm glad to know that y'all didn't and don't care about my stutter. Thank you for your not allowing my stutter impact my job or your view of me being able to do my job. Thank you for your willingness to talk to me about stuttering and how it impacts my life. Thank you for allowing me to remove any misconceptions and/or teach you about stuttering.

Regardless of when or where we worked together, thank you for seeing me and not my stutter.

Sincerely,

James

To My Teachers

Dear Teachers,

To my elementary school teachers, thank you including me in everything, regardless of my fluency. Numerous examples of this come to mind. I think of my kindergarten's annual Christmas play in which I played an inn keeper. Thank you for giving me a speaking role and allowing me to stutter through, "You are so cold." I easily could've been given a non-speaking role or excluded from the play, but I wasn't it. Looking back almost twenty years later, I appreciate being a given role and to see be seen like the rest of my classmates. I also think of my teachers who did their best to make sure I didn't miss anything critical, due to my speech therapy. Thank you for seeing my speech treatment as just as important as your class and doing your best to make sure neither suffered. I think of being allowed to participate in class, even though I stutter. That is something I know some other teachers wouldn't allow. I think of me being consoled and not pushed aside when my stutter won and kids were making fun of me for it. More importantly, thank you for encouraging me to forgive and not resent my classmates when they picked on me (fortunately I wasn't picked on that much).

To my high school teachers, thank you for allowing me to take on leadership roles in a variety of organizations. When my stutter returned during my senior year, thank you for allowing me to continue in my leadership roles on campus. Being in Big Brothers, Operation Headstart, Ambassadors, and Campus Ministry, were big parts of my high school experience and big keys in my growth as an individual. Thank you for not using my stutter as a means to discourage me from continuing in those groups. Thank you for still allowing me to give tours of the school, give talks on retreats, talk to prospective students and their parents, and representing the school at a variety of local events.

To my college professors, thank you for allowing me to set the tone of how my stutter was handled. An example that comes to mine is during the spring semester of my freshman year, I took a theatre appreciation class. For our final project, we had get into groups and write and act in a one act play. Joe, thanks for allowing me to act as if my character stuttered and I was a fluent person playing the role of someone who stuttered. I wasn't at the point where I owned my stutter and thank you for allowing me to do what was comfortable. To my public speaking professor, thank you for hearing my content and not my stutter when I presented. To my forensic professors, thank you for allowing me to pursue a field that involved testifying in court and never discouraging me to pursue this because I stutter. When I presented in class, thank you for hearing me and not my stutter.

Regardless of where you were in my educational journey, THANK YOU for not treating me any differently because of the fact that I stutter.

Sincerely,

James

Stuttering Community

To Other People Who Stutter

What's up Y'all?

First off, you are not alone. You got this. Whether you know this or not, you have a massive support system that gets it and will always be there for you. You are a part one of the most resilient communities I know. If anyone tells you differently, then they are the definition of a liar.

If you are young person and worried about how stuttering will impact your life, it will as much as you let it. Stuttering doesn't define you, but rather you define your stutter. You can do whatever you desire to do whether that is to be a scientist, CEO, athlete, actor, teacher, nurse, or whatever you wish to be.

Honestly, you care about your stutter more than others do. Yes, there will be people who make a snide comment or mock you because of it, but the majority of the people you will encounter in your life do not care about the fact that you stutter. When you encounter people who do care be mad, but more importantly be an advocate for yourself and stuttering. I know that sounds hard and it is, but you will get there in time and on your own time. Trust me. Once you accept the fact that you stutter and the fact that you care more about it than others do, life gets easier.

If you have accepted the fact that you stutter, then great! Do me a favor and advocate for others who aren't in that same boat. If you haven't accepted your stutter and hide it, that's ok! You will accept it in your own time. In the meanwhile, you have people behind you every step of the way.

Remember you have nothing to apologize for. Your stutter is just one on many things that makes you uniquely you. It does not define you. Always remember that fact.

Sincerely,

James

To the Parents of Children who Stutter

Dear Parents,

I'm here to tell you that it's **OK** that your child stutters. Yes, stuttering sucks, but it can be one of the best teachers your child will ever have. Your child is not alone in the fact that he/she stutters. There's a high chance that he/she will grow out of their stutter, but if they don't it's ok. Your child's stutter does not define him/her. Your child is so much more than his/her stutter.

My biggest tip is be there for them and support them. Encourage them to incorporate the techniques they learned in therapy into their everyday lives. If you don't, then it's a waste of time for all involved. Celebrate the small victories of stuttering with them, but remind them that they are more than their stutter when they have a bad day. Be their pair of ears when they need to vent. Don't make a big deal about the fact that they stutter because it's not a big deal. Please don't say slow down or take a deep breath when they stutter because it does more harm than good. Get involved in your local NSA chapter. It'll do more good than you can even imagine. Let them speak for themselves and you their voice. They're speaking their own language fluently.

Above all just listen and be. They'll tell you in their own time what they need and how to best help them.

Sincerely,

James

To My Speech Therapists

Dear Ms. Carol, Ms. Joan, Victoria, Hope, Amelia, and Taylor,

First off, thank you for all of the work you do not only for myself, but for others. The work you do on a day in and day out basis is more impactful than you know.

To my elementary school speech therapists, thank you for helping me go from a 5 year old kid who could barely say the letter "r" without stuttering to someone who fluently delivered the keynote speech at my 5th grade D.A.R.E. graduation ceremony. Thank you for incorporating my hobbies and interest, from The Weather Channel to *The Dumb Bunnies*, into our speech therapy sessions. Thank you for the constant encouragement and helping me become more fluent as the years passed. Thank you for compassionately listening to the troubles of a third grader. Thank you for erasing my fears that I was different from all the other kids in school.

To my college speech therapists, thank you for helping me become more fluent via the techniques I learned or re-learned from you. Thank you for being a sound board when I needed to vent about whatever was on my mind that day. Thank you for allowing me to set my goals and doing anything and everything within your power to help me accomplish those goals. Thank you for conducting our speech therapy sessions on the phone and making me call random places and ask them a series of questions. I am now far more comfortable talking on the phone because of it. You helped me achieve those goals by conducting numerous mock interviews with me, as a means of preparing for life after graduation. I am a better at interviews because of it. Thank you for making me do so many presentations to the walls of the speech therapy room, to empty classrooms, and to your classes. I am now confident in my public speaking abilities and willingly put myself into public speaking opportunities, something I never would have done if it wasn't for you. But more importantly, thank you for helping me become more confident and accepting of my stutter. Thank you for introducing me to different stuttering organizations, I would not know about them if it wasn't for you. Thank you for being a sound board and listening to me as I struggled to grapple, understand, and accept the fact that I stutter. Thank you for helping me process all of my thoughts about stuttering and helping me turn them into positives. If it weren't for the work done in the therapy room, I don't know if I would be able to accept and embrace my stutter.

Forever appreciative,

James

To Future SLPs

Dear Future SLPs,

I know that having patients who stutter is rare. I know that having adult patients who stutter is even rarer. The fact that we don't know what causes stuttering makes treating patients who stutter harder. Combine all of that and at times having a patient who stutters seems like a unicorn. With that said, you're goal in treating a patient should not be to eliminate their stutter. Your two main objectives are to them techniques to control their stutter and to help your patient improve their confidence in their voice and in themselves. Your client is so much more than his/her stutter and part of your job is to remind him/her of that.

As someone who has been through speech therapy as an elementary school student and a college student, I believe I have unique insight into what goes through the mind of your future patient. Each patient, regardless of age, is unique and has a stutter that is unique to them. Do not conform your patient to a treatment plan found in a textbook, but rather create an unique treatment plan that conforms to your patient.

When I was in speech therapy as a child, I had two great speech therapists. Not only did they help me become more fluent by teaching me different techniques to decrease my stutter, but more importantly they made it fun. They incorporated my interest into our speech therapy sessions, so it was fun and I enjoyed being there. When I first started, one of my speech therapists wrote sentences for me to practice saying and each sentence involved The Weather Channel, one of my favorite channels at the time. Other times our speech therapy sessions would involve us talking about Saints football, the book *The Dumb Bunnies*, or whatever other random topic I wanted to talk about. I enjoyed speech therapy not because I was becoming more fluent, but because it was a time where I could talk about whatever I felt like discussing.

In college, speech therapy was different. Yes, we did different techniques to decrease my stutter, but more importantly we worked on my goals and did our best to accomplish them, ultimately leading to acceptance. One of the best parts was I was able to set our goals for the semester and together we accomplished them. Setting and achieving these goals is one of the things that helped me accept the fact that I stutter.

A key thing to remember is that the word therapist is in your job title. Regardless of your patient's age, there will be days will he/she will need to vent about whatever is bothering them. Encourage them to use their techniques during these vent days, but more importantly listen to them. For me, this was key as I was going through the process of understanding, grappling, and accepting the fact that I stutter. For some patients, just being there will make a world of difference for them.

I hope this helps you and your future patients.

Thank you for what you are doing. Your job makes a world of difference in the lives of many.

Best,

James

To The NSA

Dear NSA,

To the staff, board of directors, advisory board, volunteers, and all others who support the NSA in any way possible, THANK YOU! Your hard work and dedication to the NSA is much appreciated by myself and every other member of the NSA. Every person who goes to an NSA meeting goes for different reasons, but if it were not for the work you do we wouldn't have the opportunity to attend the meetings and explore those reasons.

For the past few months, I've been asking myself why I go to the NSA meetings every first Thursday of the month. My first meeting was in October 2015. I went to see what it is all about and in hopes of continuing the progress I made in terms of accepting the fact that I stutter. Within minutes, I knew I made the right decision on going and I that I wanted to be a part of the NSA. For the first time in my twenty-two years of life, I met people who were my close to my age that stuttered. I could relate to them and them to me. I finally had people in my life that "got it".

From that first meeting a bit more than two years ago to today, I have made even greater strides towards acceptance and advocacy for stuttering. The NSA has given me many opportunities I wouldn't have had otherwise. The main one is the ability to have honest and vulnerable conversations I have had with my parents, co-workers, friends, and other members of my NSA chapter.

The main reason I go back is to answer the question my 10 year old self had which is, "Am I the only person that stutters?" The first Thursday of the month I can answer him, "You are not alone." The work you do allows myself and others to answer that same question that may have been in our minds for years. If it wasn't for the work you do, I wouldn't be where I am today.

Thank you,

James

To My Stutter

Dear Stutter,

For most of my life, you've been the friend I don't want, but couldn't see my life without. The majority of our friendship has been filled with anxiety, nervousness, hate, self-doubt, and insecurity; however, those negatives have since turned into beauty, acceptance, and ultimately self-confidence.

When we first became friends I was five. You filled me with a sense of doubt and made me wonder if I was the only person you were friends with. I went to speech therapy for seven years and as the years progressed our friendship weakened. When I went to high school, I thought you were a childhood friend that I would never see again, but wouldn't forgot. Boy, was I wrong.

We became friends again when I was a senior in high school and we've been friends ever since. Our re-newed friendship was difficult for me to accept. My senior year of high school and most of my college career was filled with a mix of self-doubt, nerves, anxiousness, and insecurities. During those years, you were winning. I didn't participate in class because I was afraid you would make an untimely visit. I had to write a script every time I wanted to talk on the phone in case it was a three way conversation between you, me, and the person on the other end. I wouldn't order through a drive thru in case you ordered something I didn't want.

My last two years of college were a time of transition for us. We went back to therapy and worked on our issues. I still didn't want you present in my life, but I began accepting our friendship. I learned ways to avoid you, but more importantly I learned how to not allow you to dictate what I could and couldn't do. I talked on the phone without a script, I started to participate in class, I volunteered for public speaking opportunities. I was allowing myself to say we are friends and not be embarrassed by our friendship.

After I graduated college and moved to a new city, you were one of the few friends I had in my new city. I still didn't want anything to do with you, but I was becoming more accepting of our friendship. Shortly after moving to my new city, we went to our first NSA meeting and it was there where I met some of your other friends. That was the best thing I've ever done because it showed me I am not the only person you are friends with, a great thing for my younger self to know. Those meetings have allowed us to be better friends and be more open about our friendship. I now openly talk about our friendship with anyone who will listen. I write about our friendship regularly and share it with whoever wants to read our story. That's something I would not have when we re-newed our friendship.

Two years have passed since we went to our first NSA meeting and our friendship has only strengthened because of it. I've accepted that we will be friends for the rest of my life and I'm okay with that. Yes, I still struggle to keep eye contact with people because I want them to look at me and not you. Your visits still cause me to wonder what the other person I am talking to is thinking about your visit. At times, I need to assure them that you're no big deal and they should ignore you.

However, our stronger friendship has also made me see the good in you. Because of you I am a better person and more confident. I see people for who they are, not what they sound or look like. I am mentally stronger and I know who I am and what I want because of you. Although at times I wish we weren't friends, I'm glad we are. I don't know where I would be without you. I guess that means I won because I see your beauty and not your ugliness.

Better luck next time,

James

Individuals

To Strangers

Dear Strangers,

I hope this letter finds you well. If you come across a person that stutters, regardless if it's every day or once in a blue moon, here are things I want you to know about stuttering and those who stutter.

First, do not finish my sentences. I know you mean well, but let me use my voice. Let me stutter and say what we want to say. It may take me few extra seconds, but what I have to say is worth saying. Unless I tell you, do not finish my sentences. This is one of the worst things you could do.

Second, do not tell me to calm down, slow down, take a deep breath, etc. Once again, I know you mean well, but please don't tell me these things. These only make me more nervous and frustrated, thus causing me to stutter more.

Third, nerves, stress, anxiety, and lack of sleep do not cause stuttering, but they don't help it. I can be stressed out and speak fluently, but be well rested and stress free and stutter on the majority of my words. I can't control when my stutter happens.

Fourth, I am not lying when we stutter. I am telling the truth in my voice, a voice that stutters. By assuming I am lying, you are doing a disservice to the person talking to you, yourself, and every other person who stutters. The person talking is telling you the truth, but lacks the confidence to tell you because of your preconceived notions. You are writing someone off without giving them a chance. You are further encouraging a stigma that people who stutter are trying their best to break.

Fifth, don't laugh or say something you think is funny. Someone stuttering is not funny and your comment isn't funny. Trust me.

Lastly, the only difference between my voice and your voice is mine takes a few extra seconds to speak.

Sincerely,
James

To The First Person to Tell Me I
Have Nothing to Apologize For

Dear Fr. Pat,

I know you may not remember this event, but I do because of the impact it had on me and my journey with stuttering.

When this event happened I was a senior in high school and my stutter had just come back. Needless to say, public speaking was not on the list of things I wanted to do. However, reading at Mass was one of the commitments I made when I joined Campus Ministry and I didn't want to avoid that commitment.

Lunchtime daily Mass had just concluded. I read the readings for the Mass and had stuttered on quite a few of the words. After Mass, I wanted to eat because lunch was halfway over, but for some reason I felt the need to apologize for stuttering during the readings. We were in the sacristy putting the chalices and ciboriums away and I turned to you and said, "Fr. Pat, sorry for stuttering during the readings." You looked at me and said, "James, you have nothing to apologize for," and continued to put away the chalices and ciboriums. That was big for me because I was a few months into my second stint of stuttering. I was heavily concerned about what people thought about my voice and how my words came out, but I didn't want to acknowledge it. Your words lifted me up and did a lot for my self-confidence.

Because of the words you said that day, I have never again apologized for stuttering nor have I let it stop me from reading at Mass. That one simple phrase rocked my world and instilled confidence into an eighteen year old stuck in a time of transition. To say I'm forever appreciative of those words is an understatement, but it's the best I can do.

Again Thank You,
James

To the Waiter Who Laughed At My Stutter

Dear Sir,

I don't remember your name, so I'll call you sir. I hope you remember this experience, but more importantly have learned from it. If for whatever reason you don't remember this experience, allow me to refresh your memory. It was the evening of October 20, 2016. I went to your establishment to have dinner with two of my cousins, who I had not seen in a while. Everything was going just fine until you asked if I wanted a refill on my drink. I responded with, "Yes," to which you responded, "What did you have?" I answered, "Un-un-un-un-unsweet tea," a response I've given numerous times to no fanfare. However, this interaction was different and resulted in some fanfare. Upon you hearing my "un-un-un," you began to smirk and chuckle to yourself. At the moment, the only people that existed in that restaurant were you and me. Knowing exactly what was going on, I gave you the ability to cover yourself by asking you, "What's so funny?" You responded by saying, "Your un-un-un-un." In a stern and matter of fact way, I responded by saying, "Yeah, I stutter." You had an "oh crap" look on your face and quickly ran off. The other patrons came back to the restaurant and my cousins and I resumed our conversation as if nothing occurred.

I write this letter not to embarrass you, but to make you realize what you did. You made fun of a person over something I have no control over. Fortunately for you, it was me who you picked on. I am confident and secure in myself and my stutter that I was able to call you out on it, be angry for a few seconds, and then move on with my life. If it was someone else, you may have destroyed their self-confidence and any progress they made in using their own voice. As for me, this experience taught me that the progress I made towards acceptance is real because I was able to call you out on it, defend myself, but more importantly let it go and not let it affect my life. Two years ago, I don't know if I could've written that previous sentence and meant it.

In closing, I hope this experience taught you something. Next time you encounter someone who stutters, be patient and let him or her say what he or she wants to say. When they finish their statement I ask you to respond with words, not laughter.

Sincerely,
James

To the Person Who Taught Me a Person Who

Stutters Can Do Great Things

Dear Joe,

When we began our weekly college bible study, I was expecting to grow only in faith and friendship. What I was not expecting was growing in confidence in my stutter. Our bible studies began a few months before I even considered going back to speech therapy and at that time you were one of the few people I would talk to about stuttering. During one of weekly meetings, we somehow got on the topic of stuttering. You casually mentioned to me that Moses stuttered, a fact I was unaware of until that moment. I was slightly taken a back and responded with a, "Oh, that's cool. I didn't know that," and we continued our weekly study. Externally I was cool, calm, and collective; however, I was freaking out internally. My mind was racing about what this factoid means and could mean for me and my life.

You see, I knew there were famous people that stuttered, but I did not know any person who stuttered that had a major impact on the world. When I heard that Moses, an individual who saved millions and a key figure in the origins of my faith, was a person who stuttered my world was rocked. Although I was nowhere close to accepting the fact that I stutter nor was it a topic I wanted to talk about, I grew a bit in self-confidence. Your comment made me realize that even though I am a person who stutters, I can still do great things in life.

Thank you for helping me realize that.

Thanks,

James

To The Person Who Thought They Were

Helping Me, But Wasn't

Dear Sir/Ma'am,

There's been many of you over the course of my life. From the waiter at a restaurant to the person on the other end of the phone to the sales clerk at the store, I know you meant well, but you weren't helping me. If anything, you were making our interaction worse. By finishing my sentence, making a snide comment, telling me to calm down and to take my time, telling me there is nothing to be nervous about, looking at me with a look of sympathy, and/or looking at me with a look of impatience, you were only further advancing the negative stereotypes and making the situation worse.

When you finished my sentences you acted as if you knew my thoughts. When you were right, you sped up the conversation and when you were wrong about my thoughts, you added time to the conversation. Regardless, you were telling me that my voice didn't matter and those few extra seconds of time were more valuable to you than what I had to say.

When you told me to calm down and take my time you acted as if you knew I what was going on in my head. I was calm and taking my time, but your words made me speed up and hurried my conversation. In that same breath, you may have told me I shouldn't be nervous because there was nothing to be nervous about. I wasn't nervous, but those words made me nervous because I was now more aware of what you thought of our interaction and how you viewed my stutter.

When you made a snide comment it was not funny, but ignorant. A joke over something I can't control says more about you than it does of me. I hope you learned from our encounter and don't do that next time you encounter someone who stutters.

When you looked at me with sympathy, impatience, or a mixture of the two, you acted as if my stutter was something to be upset about and my voice should be silenced. My stutter is not something I am ashamed or embarrassed of and you shouldn't be either. It's not something sad and requires sympathy, but something that is part of me and requires understanding. Your impatience tells me my ideas or are not worth your time and I should be silent. Sorry, but I'm going to use my voice to say what I want to say and if it takes a few extra seconds to say my ideas, then so be it. My words are just as valuable as your time.

Next time you encounter someone who stutters, I hope you just stand there while they use their voice. When someone stutters they are usually calm, not nervous, and taking their time because it can be a struggle to say what's on their mind. You're comments aren't helping the cause. Plus, people who stutter are a resilient group of individuals so you're sympathy and snide comments are not wanted nor needed. Be patient, we are just like you, but it may take us a few extra seconds to say what's on our mind.

Sincerely,

James

To the Person Who Said They Felt
Sorry For Me Because I Stutter

Dear Tim**,

First off, I don't want nor need your sympathy. The fact that I stutter is something I am not ashamed of nor embarrassed about and you shouldn't be either. In fact, my stutter is a badge I embrace and wear with pride every day.

Those of us that stutter fight an internal battle every day of if to talk, and if we choose to talk should we use our natural voice and stutter or talk in a way that hides the fact that we stutter? When we do talk with our natural voices it's because we are comfortable with who we are and who we are surrounded by. Your comment could have changed that for me, but it didn't. I am proud to say it didn't and I want on with life using my own voice in all speaking situations.

I am part of a community that is quite a resilient bunch. Every day, we fight with our stutter to determine if our stutter wins or if we win. When our stutter wins, we are quiet, may not talk, or talk in a way that hides the fact that we stutter. However, when we win, we don't care what our voice sounds like and use it freely to say what we need to say. When we win, give us encouragement, support, or best of all act like our stutter is no big deal. Sympathy is not something we need or want. I hope that sticks with you next time you encounter someone that stutters.

Sincerely,

James

** Name changed

The Future

To My Future Wife

Dear Wife,

I don't know you yet, but I can't wait to meet you, love you, and share this crazy journey we call life with you.

As you know, I stutter and probably will the rest of my life. Thank you for seeing through that and loving me regardless of it. Although I have come to embrace my stutter and wear it as a badge of honor, there will be days, very few and far between, where I wish I didn't stutter. In those days, I ask you to be there and allow me to vent about those struggles. I will be fine, but I will need to have someone there for me.

Although I cannot promise you complete fluency, I can and will promise you that my stutter will not stop be from being the best husband and father I can be. Regardless of my fluency, I will always to be there in every way possible for you and our future kids. My stutter will not stop me from getting involved in the PTA, the kid's events, making phone calls for them and you, supporting you in any venture, providing for y'all, or from anything we encounter on this crazy journey called life.

Love always,

James

To My Unborn Children

Dear Son/Daughter,

First off, I can't wait to meet you! I haven't met you yet, but I already love you immensely and unconditionally.

A fact that you need to know about me: I stutter. What that means is may take me a few extra seconds to say something. I may make some noises before I talk or my mouth might be open, but no noise comes out. When I stutter, I may not may not make eye contact with you. I'll make weird facial expressions when I stutter. Besides that, there is nothing wrong with stuttering. I am not a bad or evil person because I stutter nor am I lying. When I stutter it's not because I'm nervous, excited, or anxiety ridden. I tell you this because you may hear these things about stuttering and what causes stuttering. I want to tell you that all of those are wrong. Stuttering is just something that happens when I talk. There is nothing wrong with stuttering. My stutter has taught me numerous lessons and given me opportunities I could never have imagined.

With that said, I hope you do not stutter. I say this not because it would affect how I love you or how much I love you because it won't, but out of love for you I don't want you to go through what I went through. I don't want you to be filled with self-doubts every time you talk. I don't want you to be afraid of or avoid speaking out in class, talking on the phone, and ordering your meal at a restaurant. I don't want you to be constantly thinking about what the person on the other side is thinking about you and your stutter. I don't want you to be picked on in school because of your stutter. I don't want people to think you are dumb, lying, or a bad person because you stutter. I don't want you to experience the self-doubts and insecurities I went through.

But if you do stutter, great! You have someone that I didn't have in my life, which is someone close in your life who gets what it means to stutter and all of the mental and emotional "stuff" that comes with it. In me, you have someone who can help you and guide you through all of the stuff that stuttering brings into a person's life. There are a few things I need to tell you about your stutter. The first is: you control it, it doesn't control you. Secondly, you dictate your future, your stutter does not. Finally: you always were, always are, and always will be so much more than your stutter.

Regardless of if you stutter or not, I will always be behind you win or lose, fluent or not, on good days and bad. I will be your advocate, cheerleader, encourager, and whatever else you need. I can't wait to meet you and see the world through your eyes.

Love always,

Dad

To My Future Self

Dear James,

I'm writing this to you in the summer of 2017, right after my first NSA conference. At this conference, I heard many times that it gets better. I know this is true because my thoughts about and acceptance towards stuttering changed in college, but I still think about it when I talk. Right now, I still think about if person I am talking to you is thinking about my stutter. I have accepted that I stutter, but I still worry about if the other person has accepted the fact that I stutter. I hope the phrase "it gets better" means a bunch of things.

I hope for you that it means that you're now a retired mental gymnast. I hope it means that stuttering consumes none of your thoughts because it currently occupies some of them. I hope you continue to see the beauty in your stutter and all the ugliness is no longer thought of. I hope you no longer have days where you wish you didn't stutter. I hope you continue to not let stuttering define, but you are continuing to define it. I hope you still are involved with the NSA because it has given you so much. I hope you are advocating for stuttering and those that stutter every day and not only when you feel up to it.

I hope it gets better for you.

Yours,

James

Contact the Author:

Twitter: jameshayden48

Email: dearworldistutter@gmail.com

Website: stutteredblog.wordpress.com

For More Information about Stuttering:

National Stuttering Association: westutter.org

Stuttering Foundation: stutteringhelp.org

Made in the USA
Columbia, SC
03 June 2023

17627997R00045